Our Senses

Susan Thames

Rourke
Publishing LLC
Vero Beach, Florida 32964

www.rourkepublishing.com

PHOTO CREDITS: © Eileen Hart: title page; © Renee Brady: pages 5, 11, 13, 15, 17, 19, 21, 22; © Carmen Martínez Banús: page 7; © Thania Navarro: page 9.

Editor: Robert Stengard-Olliges

Cover design by Michelle Moore.

Library of Congress Cataloging-in-Publication Data

Thames, Susan.
Our senses / Susan Thames.
p. cm. -- (Our bodies)
Includes bibliographical references and index.
ISBN 978-1-60044-513-2 (Hardcover)
ISBN 978-1-60044-674-0 (Softcover)
1. Senses and sensation--Juvenile literature. I. Title.
QP434.T43 2008
612.8--dc22

2007011812

Printed in the USA

CG/CG

www.rourkepublishing.com – rourke@rourkepublishing.com
Post Office Box 3328, Vero Beach, FL 32964

Table of Contents

Your Senses

Can you name your
five **senses**?

Your senses and your **brain** work together.

Your senses help keep
you safe.

Your senses help you
learn things.

See

You can see with your **eyes**.

Hear

You can hear with your ears.

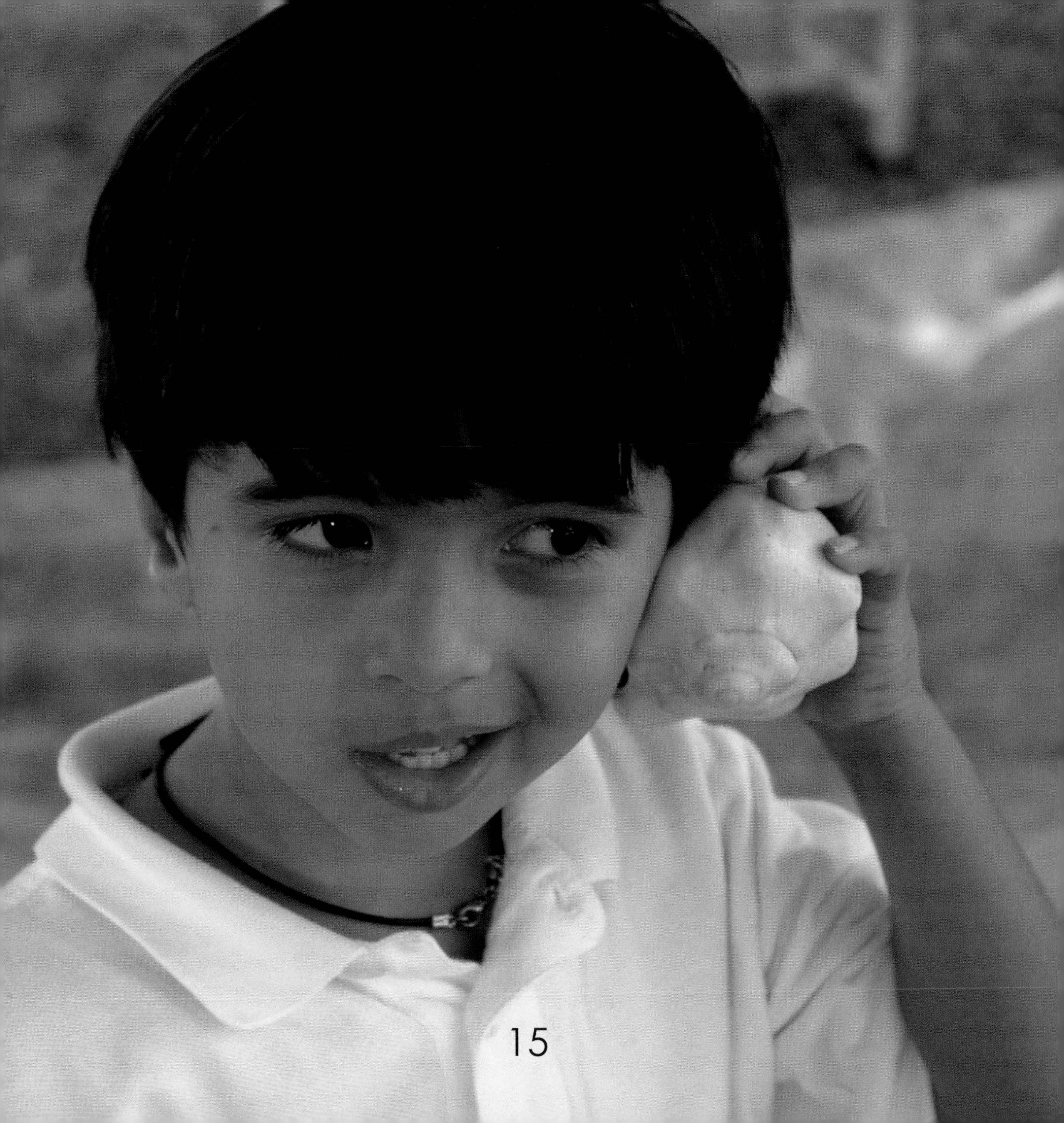

Smell

You can smell with your nose.

Touch

You can touch with your hands.

Taste

You can taste with your **tongue**.

You need all of your senses.

Glossary

brain (BRAYN) — part of the body inside the head for thinking, feeling, and controlling your body

eyes (EYEZ) — part of the body in your head that lets you see

senses (SENSEZ) — five powers you use to learn about your surroundings

tongue (TUHNG) — a part of your mouth used for tasting, swallowing, and talking

Index

Further Reading

Collins, Andrew. *See, Hear, Smell, Taste, Touch: Using Your Five Senses*. National Geographic, 2006.

Miller, Amanda. *Let's Play a Five Senses Guessing Game*. Children's Press, 2007.

Websites to Visit

www.kidshealth.org
www.healthfinder.gov/kids
www.yucky.discovery.com

About the Author

Susan Thames, a former elementary school teacher, lives in Tampa, Florida. She enjoys spending time with her grandsons and hopes to instill in them a love of reading and a passion for travel.